Welcom
Draw Your Own Adventure

I hope you like it.
Here is how to use this book.
I call this page:

INSTRUCTIONS

2. DRAW a picture. It doesn't matter if you don't think you're good at drawing. The only way to get better is with practice, right? So take your time, or scribble. It's your book. Have fun with it. Or be serious. I'm not your dad. Unless your name is Wilder Love. Then, I am your dad. But I will tell you the same thing. Have fun. And look how good I got at drawing.

Like this.

3. TURN the page. Repeat this until you're all done!

1. READ the sentence, then choose an option. Cross out the options you DON'T want to use.

Like this.

The maiden sang a song about

~~her troubles.~~
delicious quiche.
~~evil warlords.~~
~~aliens invading her planet!~~

A Knight's

Tale
Story
Saga
Elbow

Leave one.
Cross the
others out.

By Jules Fox &

_ _ _ _ _ _ _ _ _ _ _ _

This is
you.

Illustrated by

_ _ _ _ _ _ _ _ _ _ _ _

Once upon a | time / peanut / twice | **, there was a** | brave / handsome / silly / sickly | **knight.**

He fell in love with a

| beautiful |
| strong |
| smart |
| talkative |

princess.

But a
crazy
powerful
fashionable
jealous
wizard stole the princess away.

He locked her in a huge

dungeon.
tower.
mansion.
watermelon!

The knight vowed that he would rescue the princess by

April Fool's Day.
sundown.
brute force.
voodoo magic.

The people of the kingdom threw

tomatoes
money
rocks
flowers

at the knight.

The knight mounted his trusty | horse turtle lion toothbrush | **and rode into the distance.**

The knight's trusty steed grew tired, so he decided to | rest poke kiss eat | it.

The knight walked on until he met a friendly

dwarf.
goblin.
old man.
talking banana!

He told the knight to beware the powerful charms of

apples.
feathers.
underwear.
wizards.

The knight thanked him and walked carefully over a hill. swamp. lava flow. spider!

The knight arrived at the wizards secret lair and

banged on
broke down
licked
smashed through

the door.

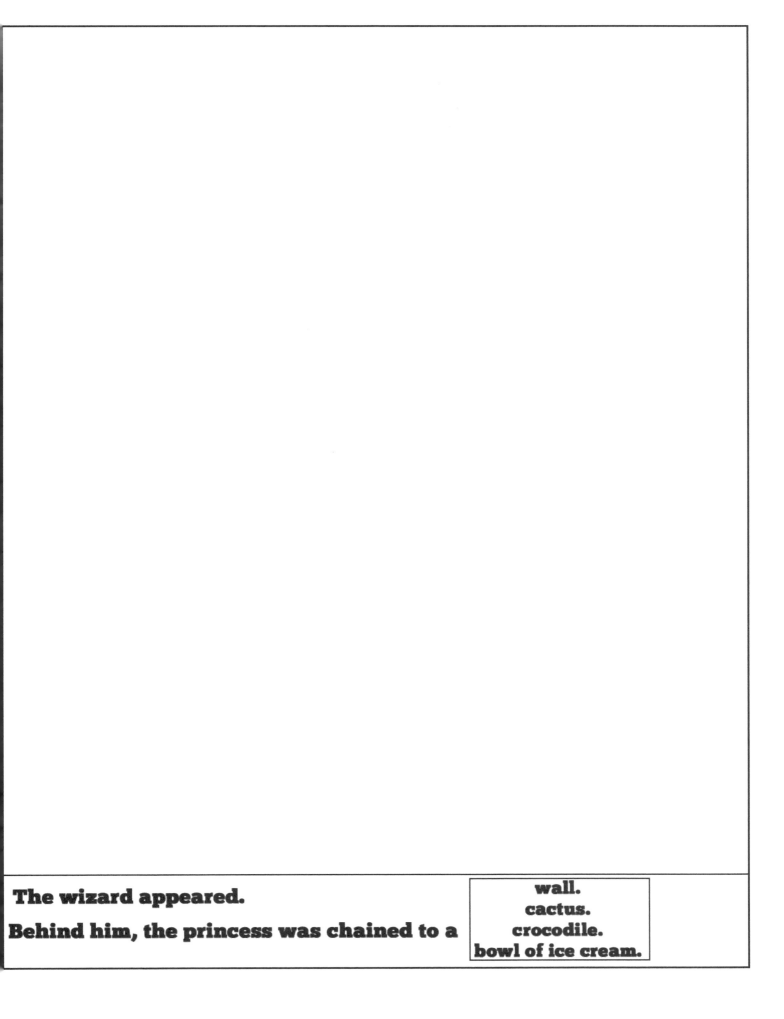

The wizard appeared.

Behind him, the princess was chained to a

wall.
cactus.
crocodile.
bowl of ice cream.

The knight let out a | sigh. scream. grunt. fart. | He said "Princess! At last I have found you."

The knight pulled out his

| sword |
| bow and arrow |
| stinky armpit |
| banana |

and attacked.

The wizard laughed and cast a

| lightning |
| ghost cats |
| giant frowny face |
| super hearts |

spell.

"The Princess is mine!" shouted the wizard as he

flew in the air.
stretched.
sneezed.
danced the cha cha!

"No" shouted the knight.
"The Princess is mine!" He

| dodged |
| hugged |
| ate |
| flipped over |

the spell.

The knight | wrestled
pushed
tickled
tricked | **the wizard backwards.**

They fell onto the Princess' chains and broke them into

tiny pieces.
a cool cloud shape.
more chains.
rose petals.

**The Princess stood up and said
"I don't belong to anyone except**

myself.
a random squirrel.
a cruel genie.
Justin Bieber!

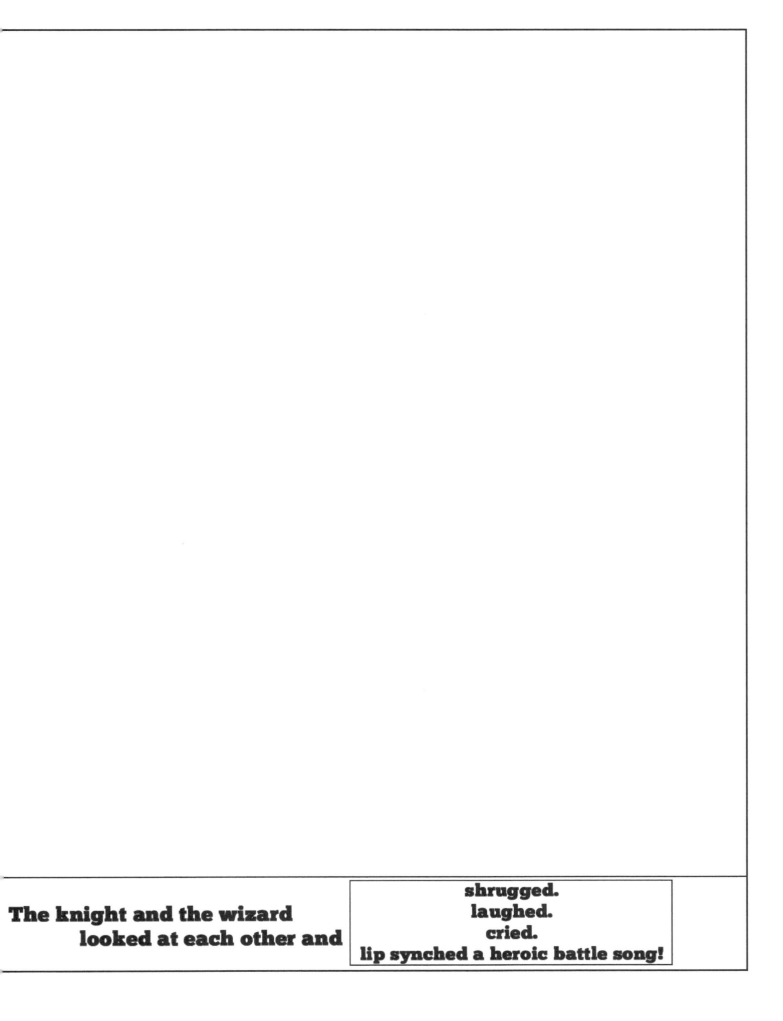

The knight and the wizard looked at each other and

shrugged.
laughed.
cried.
lip synched a heroic battle song!

"But if you had to marry one of us, who would it be?" asked the knight

longingly.
grumpily.
cheerfully.
picking his nose.

"I have made my decision," said the Princess. I will

marry the knight!
marry the wizard!
marry the village idiot!
stay single and adopt a puppy.

The sun went down and they all

lived happily ever after.
invested in real estate.
cried themselves to sleep.
went to an all day breakfast restaurant.

The

End

Sock

Fish

Baloon

If you LOVED this book, then please:
REVIEW it on Amazon and Goodreads,
TELL your friends about it,
and tell them to tell THEIR friends.

Do you want a F R E E book? Just like this one?
(But different.)
Email me at: julesdangerfox@gmail.com
and say "CABBAGES."

I will sign you up for a FREE newsletter
with FREE printable coloring pages
and FREE notifications
of when my new books come out.
PLUS of course, a FREE exclusive PDF book
That you can PRINT out
As many times as you want,
Or until your printer runs out of ink.
But then you can buy more ink,
And print more books, until you run out of money.
Then you will need to find an octopus
and squeeze it. But not too hard
because animals are awesome.
Okay bye.
Bye.
Bye for real.

- Jules

Made in United States
Troutdale, OR
11/28/2023